ICONIC NATIONAL PARKS

ACADIA NATIONAL PARK

BY LAURA PERDEW

An Imprint of Abdo Publishing
abdobooks.com

Cover image: Though Acadia is one of the smallest national parks, it is also one of the most visited.

abdobooks.com

Published by Abdo Publishing, a division of ABDO, PO Box 398166, Minneapolis, Minnesota 55439.

Printed in the United States of America, North Mankato, Minnesota.
052025
092025

Cover Photo: Shutterstock Images
Interior Photos: Edwin Remsberg/The Image Bank/Getty Images, 4–5; MiraMira/Alamy, 6; Red Line Editorial, 9, 10; Lighthouses by Allan Wood/Alamy, 11; Mike Ver Sprill/Shutterstock Images, 12; Alexey Stiop/Shutterstock Images, 14–15; Derek Davis/Portland Press Herald/Getty Images, 16; National Park Service, 20; Stan Dzugan/Moment/Getty Images, 22–23, 45; Peter Unger/Stone/Getty Images, 24; Harry Collins Photography/Shutterstock Images, 27; Hongming Zheng/500px Plus/Getty Images, 28; Shutterstock Images, 30–31; Jerry Monkman/Aurora Photos/Cavan/Getty Images, 33; Yehyun Kim/Friends of Acadia/National Park Service, 36–37; jbcn/Alamy, 39; iStockphoto, 42 (top); Chiara Salvadori/Moment/Getty Images, 42 (middle); Amy Sparwasser/iStockphoto, 42 (bottom); Lisa Wispe/Shutterstock Images, 43 (top); Anand Goteti/Cavan/Getty Images, 43 (middle); Kyle Little/iStockphoto, 43 (bottom)

Editor: Christa Kelly
Series Designer: Marley Richmond

Library of Congress Control Number: 2024948609

Publisher's Cataloging-in-Publication Data

Names: Perdew, Laura, author.
Title: Acadia National Park / by Laura Perdew
Description: Minneapolis, Minnesota: Abdo Publishing, 2026 | Series: Iconic national parks | Includes online resources and index.
Identifiers: ISBN 9781098297152 (lib. bdg.) | ISBN 9798384919674 (ebook)
Subjects: LCSH: Acadia National Park (Me.)--Juvenile literature. | Coastlines--Juvenile literature. | Natural monuments--Juvenile literature. | Scenic landscapes--Juvenile literature. | National parks and reserves --Juvenile literature.
Classification: DDC 974.1--dc23

CONTENTS

CHAPTER ONE

CROWN JEWEL OF THE NORTH ATLANTIC COAST

Yara's family stepped off Acadia's Island Explorer shuttle on the Park Loop Road. The family was at Acadia National Park in Maine. It was a couple of hours before high tide. They walked down the stone stairs toward the ocean. To the north, Yara and her brother saw Sand Beach, where they planned to go later to play in the chilly water. To the south was Otter Cliff, a granite cliff face standing 110 feet (34 m) high.

Acadia is Maine's only national park.

The best time to see big waves at Thunder Hole is two hours before high tide or during storms.

Yara and her family continued down the path. They followed it into a narrow channel on the rocky shoreline called Thunder Hole. From behind the guardrails along the path, they watched as the ocean crept into the inlet. As the tide rose, the waves splashed higher and higher. Yara held her breath, wondering what would happen next.

The tide continued to rise. Once it was at just the right level, the waves crashed into the partly submerged cave in the rocks below them. Water filled the cave with a thunderous, echoing roar as the air was forced out of the channel. Seawater sprayed 40 feet (12 m) into the air, soaking Yara and her family. They all laughed in surprise. Yara was amazed at the strength of the ocean. She was excited to continue exploring the coast with her family.

MEET ACADIA

Acadia National Park is located in Maine in the far Northeastern United States. Sometimes called the Crown Jewel of the North Atlantic Coast, Acadia protects close to

CARRIAGE ROADS

John D. Rockefeller wanted people to be able to enjoy Mount Desert Island without being in a car. Between 1913 and 1940, he funded the construction of 17 stone bridges and 57 miles (92 km) of carriage roads. The roads travel deep into the heart of the island and offer stunning views. These roads are not accessible by car. People can travel the historic roads on foot or by horse, carriage, or bike.

50,000 acres (20,000 ha) of land around the small town of Bar Harbor. The park is known for its diverse habitats, rich cultural heritage, and 60 miles (100 km) of rocky coastlines.

Acadia National Park sprawls over parts of several islands and a peninsula on Maine's mainland. Most of the park is located on Mount Desert Island. The island is connected to the mainland by a bridge. About half of the island is part of Acadia National Park.

The park's territory on Mount Desert Island is divided into

PERSPECTIVES

ACADIA'S CULTURAL HISTORY

Acadia has been home to American Indian Nations for thousands of years. The Cultural Connections in the Park program honors this heritage. Marie Yarborough works for the park. She said the program allows visitors to "learn from Maine Native people here in Acadia National Park . . . about their culture or their history . . . and what makes them feel so connected to this landscape." The hope is that visitors learn that Acadia is both a beautiful place and one with a rich cultural history.

ACADIA NATIONAL PARK

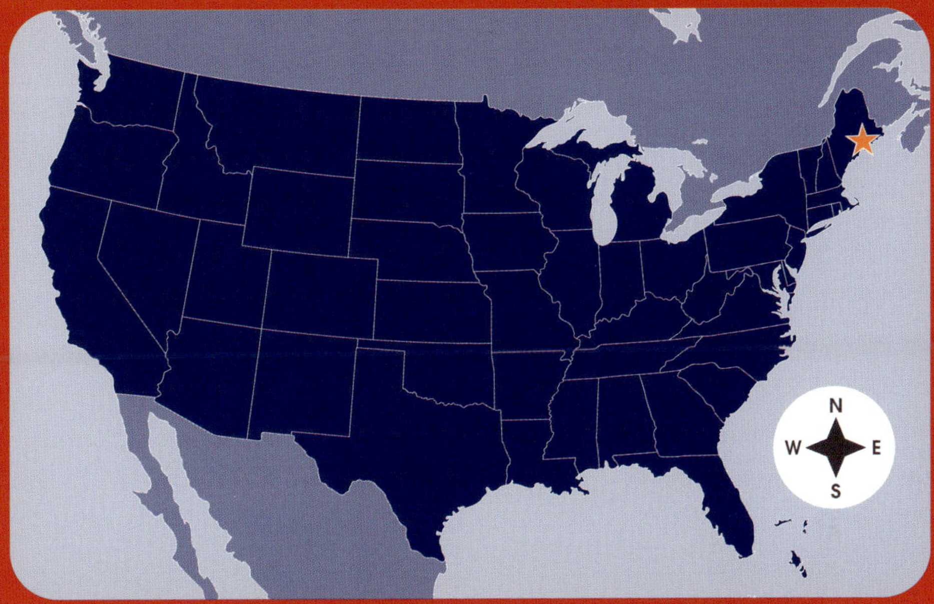

Acadia National Park is located in Maine. What do you notice about the park's location? How does this location influence the park's landscapes and wildlife?

two unconnected sides, often referred to as the east side and the west side. The east side of the park is the most popular and hosts the park's main visitor center. The west side is more secluded and perfect for quiet exploration.

Another portion of the park is located on the Schoodic Peninsula on Maine's mainland. The peninsula is about an hour from the park's main visitor center.

ACADIA
NATIONAL PARK

Acadia National Park is spread across more than a dozen islands. How might this make the park more difficult to maintain? Why do the islands need to be protected?

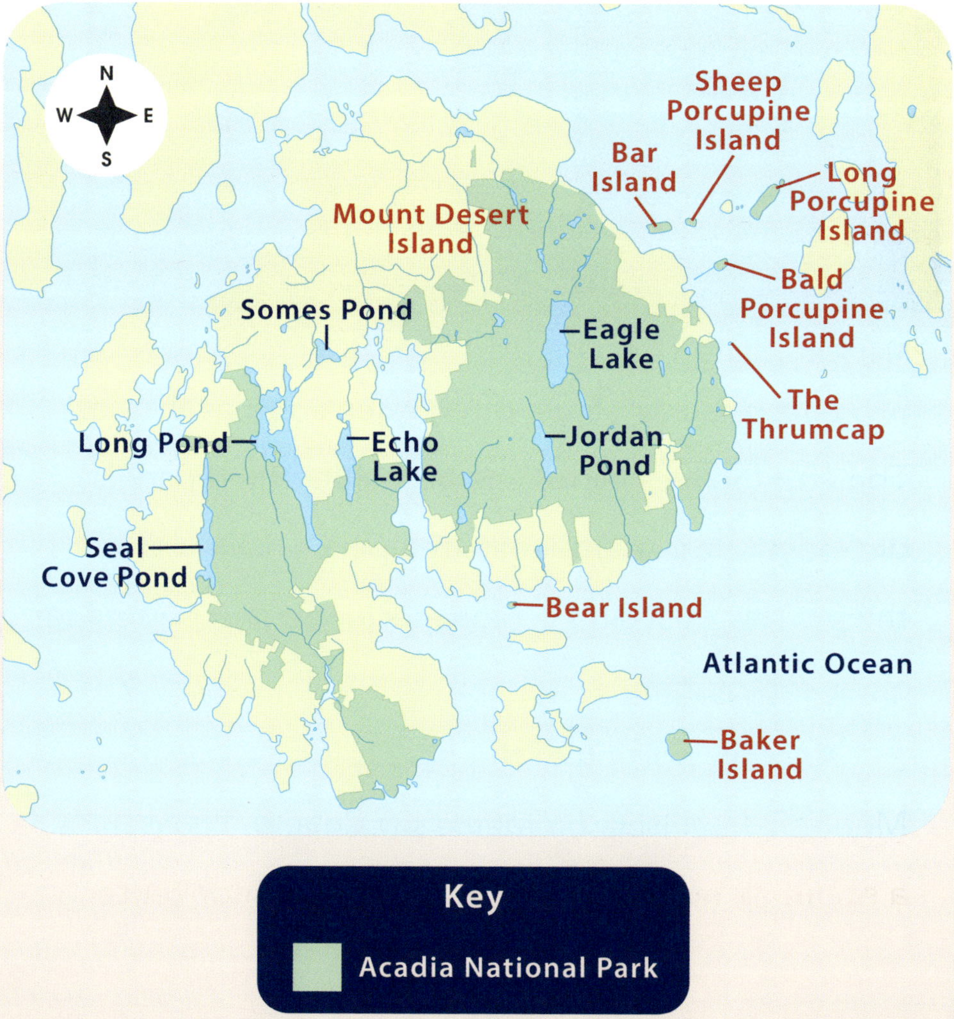

N
W
E
S
Sheep Porcupine Island
Bar Island
Long Porcupine Island
Mount Desert Island
Bald Porcupine Island
Somes Pond
Eagle Lake
The Thrumcap
Long Pond
Echo Lake
Jordan Pond
Seal Cove Pond
Bear Island
Atlantic Ocean
Baker Island
Key
Acadia National Park

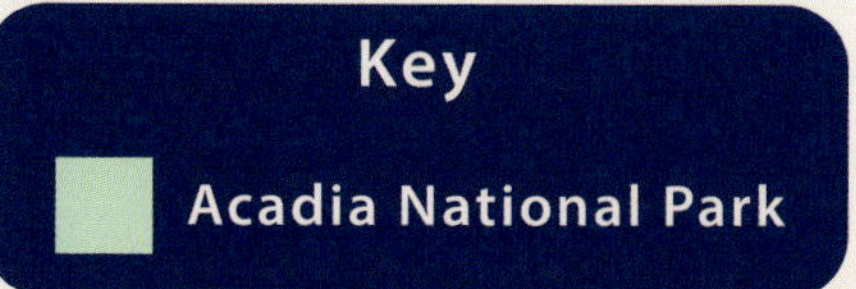

Many of Acadia's islands, such as Bear Island, are closed to the public but can be viewed by boat.

The rest of the park is spread across more than a dozen islands, though only three are accessible to the public.

ACADIA'S ATTRACTIONS

Mount Desert Island's Park Loop Road offers visitors a scenic drive through the east side of the island.

People can hike down to Jordan Pond or take a trail to an overlook for a breathtaking view of the water.

The 27-mile (43 km) road takes visitors to some of the park's most popular attractions, including Sand Beach and Thunder Hole. The road also brings visitors to Cadillac Mountain, the highest point in the park. The mountain rises 1,530 feet (470 m) above sea level. Visitors can drive to the top of the mountain for a stunning view of the park and the Atlantic Ocean.

Southwest of Cadillac Mountain is Jordan Pond. Next to this beautiful pond is the Jordan Pond House, where guests can stop for a bite to eat. The house has served guests since the late 1800s.

Acadia's rugged beauty and vast variety of wildlife make it one of the most visited national parks in the United States. Four million people visit the park each year, eager to see one of the most beautiful places on the East Coast. The park's captivating landscapes and fascinating history offer something for each visitor to enjoy.

EXPLORE ONLINE

This chapter is an introduction to Acadia National Park. Watch the video at the website below for a virtual tour. The narrator refers to Acadia as a friend. How does Acadia become a friend to visitors? How does this perspective add to the information in Chapter One? What new information did you learn?

ACADIA ALWAYS

abdocorelibrary.com/acadia-national-park

CHAPTER TWO

HISTORY OF ACADIA NATIONAL PARK

Acadia's geologic history stretches back more than 500 million years when the area's oldest rocks were formed by heat and pressure deep underground. Other types of rocks formed from sedimentation, volcanic ash, and magma. Over time, these rocks were shaped and moved by glaciers, volcanic activity, and other natural forces. These forces created the rounded mountaintops and rugged shorelines visible today.

Acadia has more than 20 mountains.

Today, nearly 8,000 Wabanaki people live in Maine.

American Indians have inhabited the Acadia region for 12,000 years. This area is the homeland of the Maliseet, Mi'kmaq, Passamaquoddy, and Penobscot Nations. Together, these nations are known as the Wabanaki, a name translating to "People of the Dawnland."

The Acadia region provided the Wabanaki people with everything they needed. They gathered berries and clams for food. They hunted fish and other prey. Tools were built from stones, clay, and animal bones. Craftspeople wove beautiful baskets from ash trees and sweetgrass. Many Wabanaki still practice this art form today.

LIGHTHOUSES

Due to Acadia's oceanside location, lighthouses are an important part of its history. Lighthouses are sources of light that sailors use for navigation. Today, the park manages three lighthouse stations, each more than 150 years old. Each station includes a lighthouse tower and light, a place for lighthouse keepers to live, a boathouse, a fuel house, and a signal station. The insides of the lighthouses are not open to the public. However, visitors can take guided tours of the outsides of some of the stations or view them by boat.

EUROPEAN ARRIVAL

European explorers first visited the area in the 1500s. There is little recorded information until French explorers came to Mount Desert Island in 1604. One explorer, Samuel de Champlain, described the island as bare and rocky.

He named it Isles des Monts Déserts, or "Island of the Bare Mountains."

Many French people settled in the Acadia region. However, the French weren't the only explorers who wanted to claim the land. The British fought the French for the land for 150 years until England finally took control in the mid-1700s.

British settlers tried to force the Wabanaki people from their homelands. When the Wabanaki resisted, the settlers murdered many of the native people. Others were killed by European diseases. More settlers arrived in the 1800s and established farms, lumber mills, and fishing businesses, further displacing the native people.

TOURISM AND ACADIA NATIONAL PARK

In the 1800s, tourists began to visit the Acadia region. Though the available lodging and food were simple, people were drawn by the area's rugged beauty. Those who came to the island for a rustic experience were called rusticators. They enjoyed the fresh salt air and the quiet pace of Maine life.

Powerful and wealthy families built huge summer homes on Mount Desert Island during this time. These families played key roles in protecting the land. In 1901, a man named George B. Dorr established an organization to acquire donated land to protect the area from overdevelopment and logging. Dorr fought tirelessly for years for the land to become a national park.

PERSPECTIVES

GEORGE B. DORR

George B. Dorr first visited Mount Desert Island as a teenager in 1868. He enjoyed nature and grew to love the island. When he became an adult, he moved onto the island permanently. He spent the rest of his life working to acquire land to preserve the area's natural beauty. When describing the area, Dorr said, "Everywhere there is life, spreading mats of crowberry and the beautiful coast juniper. . . . Few forests in the world . . . clothe themselves with such abundant life, and there are none that bring one more directly into touch with nature, its wildness and its charm."

George B. Dorr is often known as the Father of Acadia National Park.

In 1919, Dorr's efforts paid off, and Acadia was designated a national park. Originally named Lafayette National Park, the name was changed to Acadia in 1929. Today, as a result of land donations and insightful stewardship, Acadia is still very much like it was when it became a national park more than 100 years ago.

STRAIGHT TO THE SOURCE

The Abbe Museum in Bar Harbor, Maine, teaches visitors about Wabanaki history and culture. The main exhibit, *People of the First Light*, shares 12,000 years of Wabanaki history. It was created in collaboration with the Wabanaki nations. Some of the displays in the exhibit explore the impact white settlers had on the Wabanaki people. One display states:

> *Decolonization is broadly defined as the process of reversing colonialism, both politically and culturally. It involves not only recognizing Indigenous perspectives and the ongoing colonization of Indigenous nations, but the devastating effects that colonialism has on Indigenous cultures.*

Source: "People of the First Light Main Exhibit Text." *Abbe Museum*, n.d., abbemuseum.org. Accessed 30 Jan. 2024.

WHAT'S THE BIG IDEA?

Read this quote carefully. What is the main idea? How is it supported by details? Why is decolonization important to many Wabanaki people?

CHAPTER THREE

PLANTS AND ANIMALS

Acadia National Park is known for its beautiful, diverse habitats. The park contains mountains, meadows, woodlands, lakes, streams, shorelines, and ocean waters. These habitats give the park its unique landscape.

Each of the park's habitats is home to a wide range of plant and animal species. This biodiversity is partially due to the park's location. Acadia is located in the transition zone between the northern boreal forest and

Acadia National Park is teeming with life in its woods, waters, and skies.

Park visitors can see more than 400 of Acadia's native plant species in the Wild Gardens of Acadia.

the eastern deciduous forest. This means that the park is home to plants and animals common in both regions, providing a unique mix of species.

PARK PLANTS

More than 1,100 different plant species can be found in Acadia National Park. Among the most prominent plants in the park are the towering trees. Acadia has both deciduous and coniferous trees. Common deciduous trees in the park include maple, oak, and birch. The leaves of these trees change colors in the autumn before falling to the ground. Mixed among these trees are conifers such as cedar, spruce, and pine trees. These trees have needles that remain green year-round.

Acadia also has lush greenery. Ferns grow in cool, shady areas with a lot of moisture. The park also has stunning wildflowers. Lily of the valley and bunchberry thrive in the woodlands. Milkweed, goldenrod, and wild strawberries sprout alongside various species of grasses, filling the meadows with bright colors.

ACADIA'S ANIMALS

The plants in Acadia provide food and shelter for a variety of wildlife, from burly black bears to microscopic organisms. Acadia is especially well known for its bird populations. More than 300 different species of

PERSPECTIVES

BARBARA PATTERSON

Barbara Patterson was passionate about birds. In 1957, she began birdbanding and collecting information about Acadia's migratory songbirds. Over more than 20 years, Patterson banded nearly 30,000 birds. Today, Patterson's work helps Acadia's scientists assess changes in bird activity. One park official said, "What is astounding is her meticulous organization of individual records for each bird that was banded. It represents not only an unrelenting dedication to high professional standards but an uncanny understanding that this information would someday be of immense importance to the conservation of birds and the habitats they used during migration."

birds can be found in Acadia. Many are migrating songbirds and raptors that return every year to breed. Others stop in Acadia during yearly migrations. The park provides these travelers with food and safe places to rest during their journeys.

Other birds live in the park for most of the year. Ospreys, gulls, sandpipers, and many other shorebirds live near Acadia's rocky shores. Mergansers and loons spend their

Several species of owls live in Acadia, including barred owls.

days near the park's lakes, and bald eagles can be seen soaring over Acadia's cliffs. Owls and woodpeckers populate the park's forests, while herons live in the wetlands.

Acadia is home to about 40 species of mammals. Among Acadia's mammals are eight species of bats. The park's bats come out at night to hunt insects. White-tailed deer, porcupines, flying squirrels, and

Visitors to Acadia National Park may see several species of whales, including humpback whales.

several species of mice live in the park's forests. These animals provide food for a number of carnivores, including foxes, raccoons, bobcats, and minks.

There are only seven species of reptiles in the park. Acadia is home to two types of turtles and five types of snakes. The park also hosts 11 species of amphibians. These animals include six species of frogs, four species of salamanders, and the American toad.

The oceans of Acadia are home to a variety of marine life. Some are large mammals, such as whales, harbor porpoises, and seals. Fish, crustaceans, squid, and octopuses inhabit Acadia's waters too. Some live in deep ocean waters, while others inhabit tide pools on the park's shores.

TIDE POOLS

Tide pools dot Acadia's rocky shores. At high tide, the ocean washes across the rocks. As the tide recedes, some water remains in holes along the coast, forming tide pools. These pools are little ecosystems. Some of the organisms in tide pools are too small to see without a microscope. Other organisms are larger, such as crabs, sea stars, and sea snails. Some of these organisms are visitors and leave when the tide returns. Others, such as barnacles and kelp, stay in the tide pools permanently.

CHAPTER FOUR

RECREATION

Many people come to Acadia to hike. One of the park's most unique hikes is the journey to Bar Island. For an hour and a half before and after low tide, a gravel bar is exposed, creating a land bridge between Mount Desert Island and Bar Island. Once on Bar Island, people can explore tide pools, hike up the trail into the forest, and take in views of Bar Harbor and the bay. Anyone who goes out to the island must pay attention to the tides. When the tide

Many of Acadia's trails allow hikers to bring their dogs.

A WINTER VISIT

Most people visit Acadia National Park in the summer, but there is still plenty for visitors to do in the winter. While some roads are closed, others remain open for scenic drives. Coastlines are open to explore too. The park also offers winter recreational activities such as skiing and snowshoeing on the park's carriage roads. Best of all, there are few crowds in the winter.

comes back in, the land bridge is once again covered in water.

There are many other hiking trails for Acadia's visitors to explore. The park has more than 150 miles (240 km) of trails. The trails wind through a variety of habitats. Some follow the shoreline, while others take hikers inland through forests and along lakeshores.

SEASIDE ACTIVITIES

Acadia's seaside location and many lakes make it an excellent place for water recreation. Some visitors paddle the coastline or lakes by kayak or canoe. Others take boat tours.

Jordan Pond's clear water makes it an excellent place to kayak.

Getting out on the ocean is also a great way to see marine wildlife. Visitors can look for puffins and seals. Tourists should always stay a safe distance away from wildlife, so binoculars are recommended for getting a closer view.

RANGER PROGRAMS

Visitors interested in learning more about Acadia can attend a ranger program. During the day, rangers offer guided walks and bike tours where they teach visitors about the park's plants, animals, and history. In the evenings, rangers host campfire talks. These interactive

PERSPECTIVES

BIRD-WATCHING IN ACADIA

Some people consider Acadia one of the best places in the country for bird-watching. The park is home to hundreds of species of birds, including more than 20 species of warblers. American ornithologist Roger Tory Peterson once called Mount Desert Island "the warbler capital of the world." Other renowned ornithologists have also spent time in Acadia. Many have conducted research on the park's birds that has helped scientists understand how birds interact and share habitats.

evening programs are especially fun for families with children. Other evening programs include activities such as stargazing.

Acadia also has dedicated centers for teaching visitors about the park. Visitor centers offer exhibits about Acadia's natural and human history. The Schoodic Institute on Schoodic Peninsula is another great resource. The institute partners with the park to teach visitors about science and conservation.

STRAIGHT TO THE SOURCE

Every park in the National Park System creates a foundation document to guide the management of the park. Acadia National Park's purpose statement is part of the park's foundation document. It says:

> *Acadia National Park protects [ecosystems], cultural history, scenic beauty, and scientific values within the Acadia [region] and offers visitors a broad range of transformative and inspiring experiences among the park's diverse habitats, glacially sculpted mountains, and bold, rocky coastline.*

Source: "Foundation Document: Acadia National Park." *National Park Service*, Sept. 2016, nps.gov. Accessed 23 Sept. 2024.

BACK IT UP

Read Acadia's purpose statement closely. Write a paragraph describing the point the statement is making. Why is this purpose statement important?

THERESE PICARD
US
PARK RANGER
799
MOTOROLA
BODYCAM

CHAPTER FIVE

CARING FOR THE PARK

People have cared for the Acadia region for thousands of years. Today, the park is managed by the National Park Service. The park service works in partnership with American Indian nations, scientists, and conservation groups to keep the park's ecosystems preserved for future generations.

Visitors can also help preserve Acadia. Park rangers say that the best way to preserve the park is to limit visitor impacts. This means

About 90 workers are employed at Acadia year-round to protect the region and educate visitors.

properly disposing of all trash, staying on designated trails, and taking extra caution with campfires. Visitors are also asked to not collect shells, rocks, or wildflowers.

PERSPECTIVES

CIVILIAN CONSERVATION CORPS

Some of the earliest efforts to care for Acadia took place when it was still a young park. During the Great Depression, a group called the Civilian Conservation Corps (CCC) was established to complete public works projects. The park's superintendent, George B. Dorr, requested the CCC's help to make Acadia more accessible. The CCC worked in the park for nine years. During that time, it created hiking trails throughout the park, constructed campgrounds, and more. The legacy of the CCC is evident to Acadia's visitors today.

REDUCING VISITOR IMPACT

Even when visitors follow the park rules, tourism affects the park. However, the park service takes steps to reduce visitor impact. One way rangers minimize visitor impact is by providing free shuttles for tourists. During busy

The first Island Explorer buses were introduced in 1999.

seasons, the Island Explorer buses take passengers to popular areas. This reduces traffic and pollution while also providing a relaxing way to get around the park.

However, some visitors prefer to drive. The park limits traffic by restricting the number of cars at popular areas at any one time. Park rangers occasionally limit foot traffic too. Trails in the park are sometimes closed to protect wildlife. For example, peregrine falcons nest in the park in the spring. To avoid disturbing the birds, trails near the birds' nests are closed during nesting season.

NIGHT SKY

In many parts of the world, light pollution makes the sky too bright to easily see stars. This light pollution also impacts wildlife. Migrating birds and animals need dark skies to hunt and hide. Acadia's Night Sky Initiative was started to protect the park's dark skies and educate the public about the importance of limiting light pollution. The park has installed light fixtures that minimize impact. Visitors are encouraged to turn off car lights and flashlights unless needed. This allows people to see the park's brilliant stars.

CLIMATE CHANGE

Climate change is one of the biggest threats facing Acadia. Human activity is causing temperatures to rise, both on land and in the water. This is endangering Acadia's native species, many of which won't be able to survive the rising temperatures.

Acadia's park rangers are doing their best to protect the park from climate change. They have adopted a new conservation approach called RAD. This acronym stands for resist, accept, and direct. The park is undergoing many changes. Acadia's park rangers must choose whether to resist, accept, or direct each change. Resisting changes means to push back against the effects of climate change. Accepting changes means to let certain effects happen. Directing changes means to allow the change to occur but to alter the ecosystem to be less impacted by the change. With the help of the park's visitors, park rangers can use these tactics to protect Acadia and preserve its beauty for future generations.

FURTHER EVIDENCE

Chapter Five discusses many ways to care for Acadia National Park. Visitors have a role in that responsibility. How can visitors minimize their impact on the park? Visit the website below to learn about the Leave No Trace Seven Principles. How do the principles protect parks?

LEAVE NO TRACE

abdocorelibrary.com/acadia-national-park

PARK LANDMARKS

Cadillac Mountain is the highest point in Acadia National Park. It offers stunning views of the coastline and beyond.

Sand Beach has a large sandy beach where visitors can relax and swim in the chilly ocean.

Schoodic Institute partners with Acadia National Park to teach visitors about the region. The institute offers educational programs.

Thunder Hole is located on Mount Desert Island. At certain tide levels, waves crash into the narrow channel, creating a thunderous sound.

Jordan Pond is one of Acadia's many pristine lakes. People can explore the lake and visit the historic Jordan Pond House for a bite to eat.

Pemetic Mountain is the third-highest mountain in Acadia National Park. People can hike to the mountain's summit to see gorgeous views of the park.

STOP AND THINK

Say What?

Studying national parks can mean learning a lot of new vocabulary. Find five words in this book you've never heard before. Use a dictionary to find out what they mean. Write the meanings in your own words, and use each word in a new sentence.

Surprise Me

Chapter Three discusses the plants and animals of Acadia National Park. After reading this book, what two or three facts surprised you? Write a few sentences about each fact. Why did you find each fact surprising?

Dig Deeper

After reading this book, what questions do you still have about Acadia National Park? With an adult's help, find a few reliable sources that can help you answer your questions. Write a paragraph about what you learned.

Why Do I Care?

Maybe you won't ever travel to Acadia. But that doesn't mean you can't take action to care for the places near you. In Chapter Five, you learned about how people are caring for Acadia. What did you learn that you can apply to a place near you? How can you conserve the area? What choices can you make in your everyday life that might indirectly benefit the area?

GLOSSARY

birdbanding
placing a numbered band on a bird's leg to identify the bird

colonization
the process of taking control of an area

ecosystem
a community of organisms living together and interacting

geologic
related to the study of the earth and rocks

habitat
the natural home of a plant or animal

migration
a seasonal movement from one area to another

organism
a living thing

ornithologist
a person who studies birds

peninsula
an area of land surrounded by water on three sides

sedimentation
a natural process during which small bits of sand, stone, and other particles settle and form rocks

ONLINE RESOURCES

To learn more about Acadia National Park, visit our free resource websites below.

Visit **abdocorelibrary.com** or scan this QR code for free Common Core resources for teachers and students, including vetted activities, multimedia, and booklinks, for deeper subject comprehension.

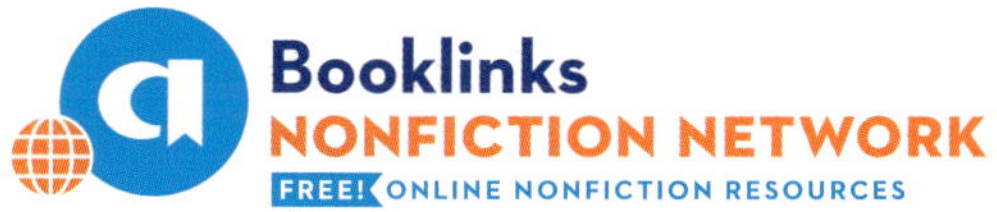

Visit **abdobooklinks.com** or scan this QR code for free additional online weblinks for further learning. These links are routinely monitored and updated to provide the most current information available.

LEARN MORE

Lassieur, Allison. *The National Parks Encyclopedia*. Abdo, 2023.

Ward, Alexa. *America's National Parks*. Lonely Planet, 2024.

INDEX

About the Author

Laura Perdew is an author coach, presenter, former teacher, and the author of dozens of fiction and nonfiction books for kids. Her books highlight the wonders of nature and call for action to preserve it. She lives in Boulder, Colorado.